HAPPY NEW YEAR!

BY
Emery Bernhard

ILLUSTRATED BY
Durga Bernhard

LODESTAR BOOKS
Dutton   New York

Library of Congress Cataloging-in-Publication Data

Bernhard, Emery.
   Happy New Year!/by Emery Bernhard; illustrated by Durga
Bernhard.—1st ed.
      p.   cm.
   Summary: Describes the origins of New Year traditions and ways
in which the coming of the new year is celebrated around the world.
   ISBN 0-525-67532-9
   1. New Year—History—Juvenile literature.   2. New Year—Cross-
cultural studies—Juvenile literature.   [1. New Year.
2. Festivals.]   I. Bernhard, Durga, ill.   II. Title.
GT4905.B38   1996
394.2'614—dc20   95-25572   CIP   AC

Published in the United States by Lodestar Books,
an affiliate of Dutton Children's Books,
a member of Penguin Putnam Inc.
375 Hudson Street, New York, New York 10014

Published simultaneously in Canada
by McClelland & Stewart, Toronto

Editor: Rosemary Brosnan   Designer: Barbara Powderly
Printed in Hong Kong   First Edition   10 9 8 7 6 5 4 3 2

On the title page:
A costumed lion is often seen in Chinese New Year street processions.

to Leslie, John,
and baby Nile—
born on the eve of
the New Year.

The snow is melting in the warm April sun. Robins chirp and hop about, searching for worms. There is a splash of color on the ground—the first wildflowers—something we have not seen for months.

Every year, we know spring will come, but after a long winter, signs of spring are a joyous sight!

Long ago, people were not always sure that winter would end and that another growing season would begin. They thought that various gods had the power to make a gift of a fertile earth and a new year. It was believed that the sun might not return or the earth might not grow plants again without the help of the gods. They performed rituals and made offerings to gain the gods' favor. Then, like a miracle, the warm, sunny days and gentle showers of spring brought the world to life!

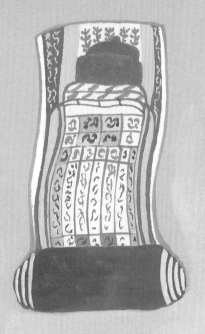

ISLAMIC SCROLL CALENDAR

ANCIENT CELTIC CALENDAR

ANCIENT EGYPTIAN PROCESSION
OF THE GODS, EACH REPRESENTING
A PHASE OF TIME

TWELFTH CENTURY
CHRISTIAN CALENDAR

People all over the world welcome the new year. For everyone, it is a time of hope for the future.

Different cultures measure time in different ways. The dates for New Year's celebrations vary from place to place and have changed through the ages.

AZTEC CALENDAR

In ancient times, the Greeks celebrated the New Year on the shortest day of each year—which we now call winter solstice—when a feast was held for Kronos, god of time. Kronos holds a sickle for harvesting everything that lives and grows.

Calendars have been based on the cycles of the sun, the phases of the moon, and the movements of the stars. People have also marked time with the changing seasons and the planting or harvesting of crops. Some cultures had annual calendars that began and ended on the shortest or longest day of the year or when the days and nights were of equal length.

Thousands of years ago, the Druids in the British Isles watched the position of the sun and the phases of the moon to find out when their year was over. Then, at the end of what we now call October, they began their new year.

Every New Year, we take part in the oldest of all festivals.

How do different cultures celebrate the New Year?

What do the various New Year's holidays have in common?

At midnight on December 31—New Year's Eve—thousands of people in the streets and millions of television viewers around the United States watch the slow descent of a large, lighted ball over Times Square in New York City. The ball weighs more than two hundred pounds and is lowered down a tall flagpole by cables. Everyone cheers the moment the ball reaches the bottom!

Those of us who celebrate New Year's Day on January 1 are using the calendar introduced by the Roman emperor Julius Caesar about two thousand years ago. The date of the Roman New Year was originally in the spring, close to the time of year when day and night are equal—called equinox.

January—the first month—was named after Janus, the Roman god of beginnings and endings, of planting and harvesting. In ancient Rome, the people gathered before the temple of Janus on New Year's Day to feast and give thanks. They also exchanged gifts and wished one another peace in the year to come.

The god Janus had two faces. One face looked back at the old year. The other face looked forward to the new year.

Romans today have various ways of celebrating the New Year. Along with giving gifts and feasting, it is customary to get rid of the old and make way for the new. At midnight, many families throw all their cracked or chipped crockery out the window. Anyone passing by below must watch out!

In many places, seeing out the old year is as important as seeing in the new one. This tradition grew from the primitive belief that, as the year weakened and died, evil spirits grew stronger and more dangerous. These demons had to be scared off before a new year could be born—often with a great deal of noise!

Noise-making has always been a part of New Year's activity. People beat drums and tin pans, blow whistles and horns, clang gongs, ring church bells, explode firecrackers, or simply shout out loud.

Cowboys in the Wild West of nineteenth-century United States rode into town to celebrate on December 31. They began a tradition of going into the streets at midnight to fire their pistols in the air.

Noise-making on New Year's Eve is still a serious business in places like Bali. During the spring equinox, the Balinese feast and make elaborate offerings to the gods. Each village parades a huge papier-mâché demon. People ignite firecrackers and play drums and gongs to drive away evil spirits before the new year begins.

The first day of the new year is a day of silence and peace when everyone stays home and does as little as possible.

Ibo children in the countryside of Nigeria have an important role in their New Year festival. It takes place in the spring, just as the rainy season and the planting of new crops is about to begin. As the year ends, children run into their homes and slam the doors. They must remain inside until the year is gone, for if they are caught outside, the old year might carry them off when it leaves. Finally, everyone—young and old—rushes outdoors and welcomes the new year with applause.

Russians once celebrated their New Year in the spring. In some places, winter is still burned away in the form of a straw dummy.

In Ecuador, families burn a straw man—along with a list of everyone's faults—at midnight on December 31.

Another way to say good-bye to the old year is with fire. Huge bonfires are lit in many parts of the world. Once the year has gone up in smoke, the new year can begin with a fresh start. Everyone wants to do things better next time around!

The Inuit of Alaska had a New Year tradition of chasing the evil spirits of winter into a fire when the sun reappeared on the horizon after its long absence.

New Year's Eve party-goers in nineteenth century New York City were sure to consult with Gypsy fortune-tellers who read tea leaves or looked in crystal balls.

Long ago, the Druids studied the flight of birds to foresee the future.

New Year's Day has always been a time to wonder about what the future will bring, and people have tried in various ways to predict events for the coming year.

In Colombia, there is a tradition of putting an egg in a glass of water and watching how it changes to try to see things that will happen in the new year.

Rosh Hashanah is the New Year holiday celebrated by Jews around the world. It takes place in early autumn. This "birthday of the world" is a serious but happy occasion when Jews pray for the community, wish each other a good year, and pledge to be better people in the year to come. Families go to synagogue, where the services include the blowing of the shofar, a hollowed-out ram's horn. According to the Bible, a shofar was used to summon the people to hear the Ten Commandments.

Many Jewish families gather on Rosh Hashanah for a festive meal. Among the special foods served are apples dipped in honey, to make the new year sweet.

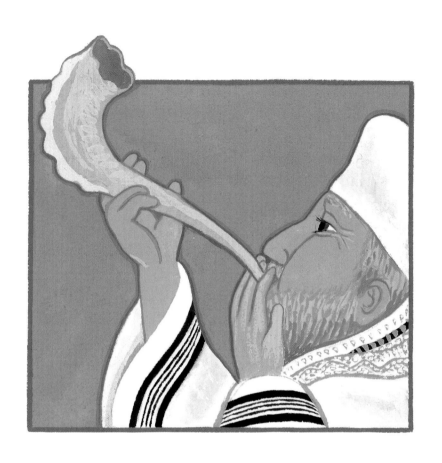

On the Islamic New Year, Muslims worship quietly. They read their holy book, the Koran, which tells how the Prophet Muhammad fled from Mecca to Medina to escape death. Many of Muhammad's followers joined him in Medina, and his flight is considered the first major event in the history of Islam.

Like Muslims everywhere, people in Egypt watch for the new moon that signals the beginning of each month. Children are especially excited by the crescent moon that starts the New Year, for on this day they receive presents and new clothes.

In some villages of the West African savannah, the new year is welcomed when the dry season ends. People clean their houses and empty all the places food is stored. Then, everyone takes turns dancing, clapping, and singing while the men drum. The songs ask the gods for a good harvest of the beans, millet, groundnuts, or sorghum that will soon be planted. Finally, the men fill gourds with water and carry them back to the village. It is their way of showing gratitude for the rains to come.

Chinese everywhere celebrate their New Year between mid-January and mid-February, which is the beginning of spring in China. It is traditionally a time for rejoicing, attending family reunions, honoring ancestors, and thanking the gods for their blessings.

On the eve of the New Year, some families in China seal the doors and windows of their homes with strips of red paper to keep out bad spirits. Then, they eat the holiday meal, which includes sweet dumplings. Children are encouraged to stay up late on this special night, and they receive good luck money wrapped in red paper. In large cities, they watch a spectacular parade. A magnificent dragon slowly weaves through the streets along with dancers, acrobats, and clowns.

The dragon that leads the Chinese New Year procession is a symbol of strength and good luck. It is made of bamboo covered with paper or silk, can be more than one hundred feet long, and may require at least fifty people to support it. The big dragon might chase anyone who teases it!

The Japanese also have a way of sealing their homes to keep out evil spirits on New Year's Eve. They hang a straw rope in front of their houses. Then they tie pine branches together and decorate them with ferns and white ribbons that stand for joy, long life, and good luck.

At mignight, gongs and temple bells all over Japan are rung again and again. Then, people begin smiling, giggling, and laughing. Everyone has been given a fresh start, and good humor is thought to bring luck in the new year!

For most of India, the new year comes in the spring. But in northwestern India, the New Year celebration takes place at the time of the Diwali Festival, on the night of November's new moon.

Thousands of small, glowing oil lamps are lit to honor Lakshmi, the goddess of wealth and prosperity. The lamps are placed in windows and doors, along roofs and porches, and are set afloat on lakes and rivers. Indians believe that wishes for the new year will come true if the floating lamps remain lit until they are out of sight. Dazzling sparklers and popping firecrackers delight children long into the night.

In Southeast Asia, the new year falls when the weather is hot and dry. Many people celebrate with water festivals. Everyone is ready for the cool, spring monsoon rains that will soon fill the rice paddies and turn the leaves green.

On New Year's Day, people walk to Buddhist temples, following the beat of the drummers who lead the way. They wash the statues of Buddha with scented water and clean the temple buildings. And—since it is believed that water can wash away all the evil deeds of the past year—people also throw bowls of water over one another!

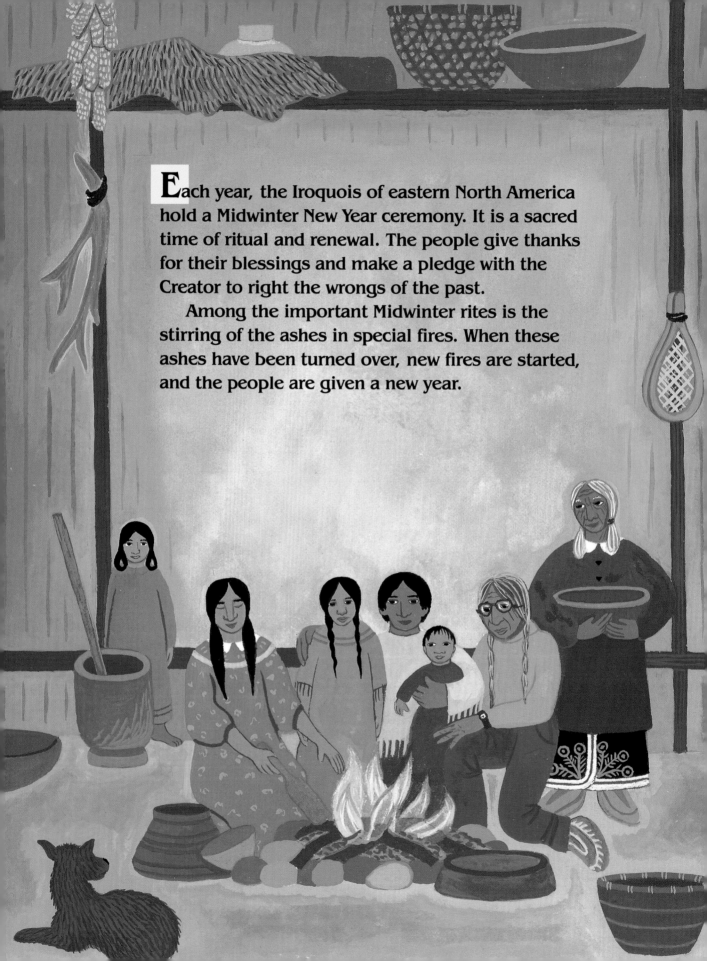

Each year, the Iroquois of eastern North America hold a Midwinter New Year ceremony. It is a sacred time of ritual and renewal. The people give thanks for their blessings and make a pledge with the Creator to right the wrongs of the past.

Among the important Midwinter rites is the stirring of the ashes in special fires. When these ashes have been turned over, new fires are started, and the people are given a new year.

The ancient Greeks worshipped the gods Kronos and Dionysus. Kronos reminded everyone that all things come to an end. Dionysus was believed to die each winter at solstice and to be reborn as a baby each spring. It is thought that the idea of the Grim Reaper—or Father Time—came from the myth of Kronos, and that the idea of the New Year Baby came from the baby Dionysus.

Something dies and something is born on each New Year. People everywhere say good-bye to the old year and feel the joy of beginning the new year. "Happy New Year!" we say, with hope for all that is to come.

HAPPY NEW YEAR!!

GLOSSARY

calendar A system for dividing time into fixed periods

Druids Members of the ancient religion of the Celts who lived thousands of years ago in western and central Europe

Dionysus God of wine and delight, in ancient Greek mythology

Ecuador Country in northwestern South America

equinox Either of the two times during the year when the length of day and night are equal

Gypsy Member of a nomadic people who probably migrated from India to Europe around the fourteenth century and who now live in Europe and the United States. Gypsies usually prefer to be called the Rom, after Romany, their language.

Inuit Native people of the Arctic regions of North America and Greenland

Mecca and **Medina** Cities in Saudi Arabia

monsoon A period of wind, especially in the Indian Ocean and Southwest Asia. Summer monsoons usually bring rain; winter monsoons are usually dry.

ritual A certain form of religious ceremony

savannah A grassy plain in hot regions

sickle A tool with a curved blade and a short handle; used for cutting grain

solstice Either of the two times of the year when the sun is farthest from the equator and does not appear to move north or south